LINKING THE PAST AND PRESENT

WHAT DID THE
VIKINGS
DO FOR ME?

Elizabeth Raum

Heinemann Library
Chicago, Illinois

H www.capstonepub.com
Visit our website to find out more information about Heinemann-Raintree books.

To order:

☎ Phone 800-747-4992

💻 Visit www.capstonepub.com to browse our catalog and order online.

Edited by Megan Cotugno and Laura Knowles
Designed by Richard Parker
Original illustrations © Capstone Global Library Limited 2010
Illustrated by Roger@KJA-artists.com
Picture research by Hannah Taylor
Originated by Capstone Global Library Limited
Printed and bound in the United States of America in North Mankato, Minnesota.
072019   002272

Library of Congress Cataloging-in-Publication Data
Raum, Elizabeth.
 What did the Vikings do for me? / Elizabeth Raum.
   p. cm. -- (Linking the past and present)
 Includes bibliographical references and index.
 ISBN 978-1-4329-3745-4 -- ISBN 978-1-4329-3752-2 (pbk.)
 1. Vikings--Juvenile literature. 2. Civilization, Modern--Ancient influences--Juvenile literature. I. Title.
 DL66.R38 2010
 948'.022--dc22
                    2009039662

Acknowledgments

The author and publisher are grateful to the following for permission to reproduce copyright material: Alamy Images p. **8** (© OJPHOTOS); The Bridgeman Art Library pp. **7** (© Nationalmuseum, Stockholm, Sweden), **21** (Private Collection); Corbis pp. **11** (Image Source), **17** (Ted Spiegel); Getty Images pp. **10** (The Bridgeman Art Library/William Gersham Collingwood), **18** (Hulton Archive), **23** (National Geographic/Peter V. Bianchi), **26** (AFP Photo/Carl De Souza), **27** (AFP Photo/Patrik Stollarz); shutterstock p. **13** (© Sally Wallis); Topfoto p. **9**.

Cover photograph of Gaia, replica Viking ship, Norway, reproduced with permission of Photolibrary/Robert Harding Travel Library.

We would like to thank Dr. Chris Callow for his invaluable help in the preparation of this book.

Contents

Look for the Then and Now boxes. They highlight parts of Viking culture that are present in our modern world.

Any words appearing in the text in bold, **like this**, are explained in the glossary.

What Did the Vikings Do for Me?

The Vikings sailed in big, wooden ships across the North Sea and northern Atlantic Ocean, in search of gold, silver, and other treasures. Wherever they landed, they attacked towns and villages. Sometimes they burned houses, churches, and **monasteries**. Vikings were fierce warriors who were feared everywhere they went.

However, violent attacks and raids were not all there was to Viking society. The men spent most of their time working as farmers. They also fished, hunted, and built boats. The women cared for their children and households. When the men went to sea, the women ran the farms. Both men and women wore jewelry and wove cloth with beautiful designs.

Look at the Viking scene below. It seems very different from modern times, but you might be surprised to discover some things the Vikings did that we still do today.

Who Were the Vikings?

About 14,000 years ago, settlers traveled west to what is now Norway and Sweden. Over time, they moved farther west and south to Denmark. Today, we call these countries Scandinavia and the people Scandinavians.

This map shows the main Viking settlements and trade routes during the **Viking Age** (800–1100 CE).

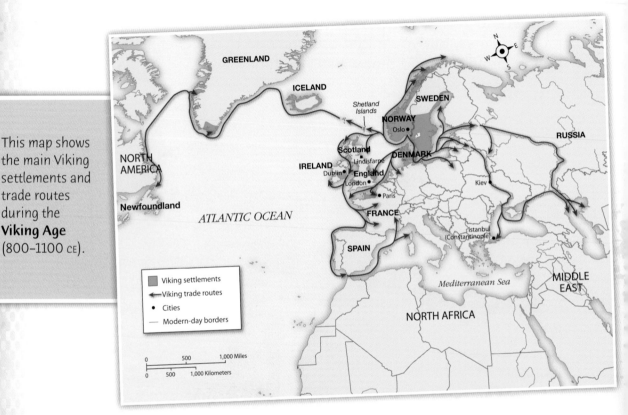

Key:
- Viking settlements
- Viking trade routes
- Cities
- Modern-day borders

0   500   1,000 Miles
0   500   1,000 Kilometers

Ancient Scandinavians

The early Scandinavians did not settle in one place. Instead, they followed reindeer and other herds so that they could hunt them. This changed in about 4000 BCE, when they began to settle down and farm the land. They had a short growing season during which they grew grains and vegetables. Cattle, sheep, goats, and pigs gave them meat and milk during the long, cold winters. They began to make metal tools, pottery, cloth, and jewelry.

All over Scandinavia, people had similar customs and beliefs. However, they began to think of themselves as different. Some were Danes, some were Norwegians, and some were Swedes. By about 500 CE, these groups traded with other Europeans.

Religion

Christianity came to Europe by 100 or 200 CE, but the Vikings kept their **pagan** beliefs for a long time. They worshipped many gods, including Odin, the god of war, and Thor, the god of thunder. Pleasing the gods was important to the Vikings. Warriors believed that if they died bravely in battle, they would live forever with Odin in his palace, Valhalla.

This painting from 1872 shows the Viking god Thor fighting giants.

Wednesday, Thursday, Friday

Three days of the week are named after Viking gods. Wednesday comes from Odin, the god of war, who was also sometimes called Woden. Thursday is named after Thor, the god of thunder. Freya, the goddess of love, gave her name to Friday.

What Was Viking Society Like?

Most Vikings were farmers. A farmer's household was made up of grandparents, parents, children, aunts, uncles, cousins, servants, and slaves.

Farms

Whole farming families lived together in a longhouse. This was a house made up of one large room, about 12–15 meters (40–50 feet) long. Sometimes one bedroom was screened off, but usually all family members slept together in one room. There was a fireplace in the middle, for warmth and cooking. Many farmers also had barns. Some farmers had a dairy and a blacksmith's **forge**.

This modern reconstruction shows what a Viking longhouse would have looked like.

THEN...

The Vikings invented ice skates. They used horse or cow bones strapped to their feet with leather. They pushed themselves across the ice with a long stick. Bone skates were slow. Skaters could only go about 4 kilometers (2.5 miles) an hour.

Transportation

Farms were often by the coast, or near rivers and lakes. During the warm months, the Vikings used boats to travel from farm to farm. When the water froze over in winter, they needed skates, skis, and sleds instead. The sleds were pulled by horses. The Vikings would fasten iron **cleats**, called frost-nails, to the horses' hooves. This meant that the horses would not slip and slide all over the ice!

Skis

Early paintings show that Viking hunters used skis to go hunting in winter. The skis were not too different from today. They were made from two curved planks with leather straps to slide the feet into.

This illustration from the 1500s shows Viking hunters using skis.

...NOW

Skates have changed a lot! Between 1200 and 1400 CE, iron began to be used instead of bone. By the 1700s, steel blades were fitted to leather boots. Today, blades are so thin and light that a good skater can go as fast as 24 kilometers (15 miles) an hour.

Kingdoms

By the beginning of the **Viking Age** (about 800 to 1100 CE), dozens of small kingdoms or chiefdoms existed throughout Scandinavia. A king would promise to protect the people from attack. In return, the people promised to be loyal to the king.

Vikings in Iceland held a yearly meeting, or *thing*, at Thingvellir, near the coast.

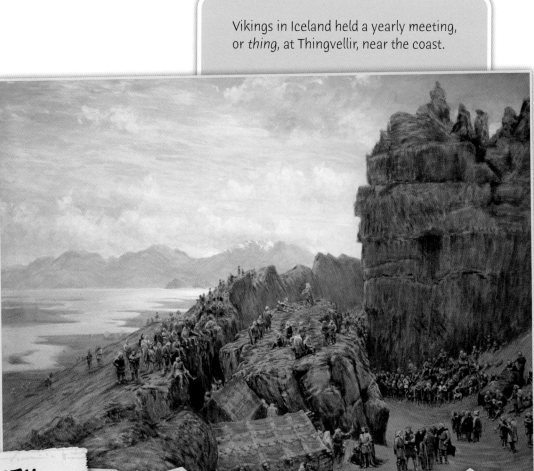

THEN...

Viking criminal trials took place at the *thing*. A group of 12 men, called a **jury**, would decide whether the accused was guilty or innocent. Occasionally the guilty were outlawed and could be killed, but usually they would only have to repay their victim.

Things

Each kingdom held a meeting once or twice a year called a *thing*. Nearly all men, except slaves, went to the meeting and many spoke there. If they were not pleased with their king, they chose a new one. They also made laws and settled arguments. Years later, the Vikings took the idea of the *thing* with them when they settled down in new lands.

Modern juries include both men and women. They include people from different backgrounds.

...NOW

The idea of trial by jury has spread to many countries around the world. Jury trials are common in the United States and the United Kingdom. However, in the United States, an accused person in a criminal trial can decide to be tried by a judge rather than a jury.

How Did the Vikings Build Ships?

In the 700s CE Scandinavia had few cities or towns. Most people lived along the coasts on large farms. They used boats for fishing and trading with one another. People from Europe visited the coastal farms, looking for furs, timber, and other goods. Sea trade with Europe grew.

Viking warships were called longships. They were fast and sturdy and could hold 60 men. The longships were carried along on the wind by sails. On days when there was little wind, the men rowed the boats through the water. Both ends of a longship were the same shape. This meant that a ship could change direction on a narrow river without having to turn around.

Viking sails were made from wool, which has a natural oil in it called lanolin. This oil made the sails waterproof.

THEN...

Viking shipbuilders used iron **rivets** (metal pins) to fasten overlapping planks, or boards, together. These **lapstrake** ships were fast, and they worked equally well in shallow or deep waters. Most boats need time to swell when they are first put in the water, or they will leak. But this is not true for lapstrake boats. They can be sailed as soon as they hit the water.

Ships used for trading were called knarrs. They were shorter and broader than a longship, and they had plenty of space to carry goods to trade. The Vikings also used knarrs to move all their belongings and animals when they settled in a new country.

Notice how the boards overlap on this modern lapstrake fishing boat.

...NOW

Wooden boat builders throughout the world continue to make lapstrake boats. Overlapping wooden boards make for fast and sturdy fishing boats, rowboats, and yachts. These boats use oars, sails, and even motors to glide through the water. Several boat-building schools throughout the world teach students to build boats like the Vikings did.

Who Were the Viking Raiders?

In 793 CE some Vikings attacked a **monastery** at Lindisfarne, an island off the northeast coast of England. They arrived in small boats, rushed ashore, and stole gold, silver, and other valuable items. They were so fierce, strong, and unbeatable that they spread fear all over Britain. This raid marks the beginning of the **Viking Age**.

Viking raiders were armed with swords, spears, and axes. They carried shields for protection. Wealthy leaders also wore iron helmets and chain mail tunics.

THEN...

While they were away, farmers depended on their wives to run the farms. They held a ceremony handing the keys to their wives. If a Viking died at sea, his wife became owner of the farm and could sell it or keep it running. If a Viking woman divorced her husband, she kept part of the household wealth. Viking law gave women property rights.

Some of these frightening fighters were full-time warriors, but many were just farmers. They left on raids in the spring, after all their crops were planted. They came home in midsummer for the harvest. Then they would set off on another raid in the fall.

While the Viking men left on raids, the women looked after the houses and farms.

...NOW

The Vikings were ahead of the rest of the world in recognizing women's rights and abilities. Unfortunately, many of those rights were lost over time. It was not until the 1800s that laws were passed in the United States and much of Europe that gave women the right to own and control property. Today, women in most countries around the world can own their own property. However, there are still many places where women are not treated equally to men.

Moving in

Viking kings grew rich from their raids. They were able to train and equip large armies. In 841 CE one of these armies landed in Ireland. It conquered Ulster and founded a settlement that would become Dublin. Instead of raiding and then returning home, as usual, the Vikings settled in Ireland. However, this did not mean they stopped raiding! Using Ireland as a base, the Vikings attacked towns, **monasteries**, and farms in Scotland and England.

In 865 CE a Viking army from Denmark invaded England. The next year, this army captured the city of York and settled there. They called it Jorvik. They built houses with thatched roofs, farmed, and set up businesses. As the population grew, they added new streets and buildings.

Craftspeople made combs, knives, jewelry, shoe buckles, leather goods, and pottery. Traders took these goods all over Europe. When they came home, the traders brought clothing, spices, and perfumes. Jorvik became a famous trading center.

Combs

Viking combs could be made from wood or bones, or deer, reindeer, and elk antlers. They could be single- or double-sided. The wealthy owned combs with delicate carvings on them, while the poor had very simple ones.

THEN...

Both English and the Viking language, called Old Norse, are Germanic languages. This means that the English and the Vikings were probably able to understand each other. Over time, the languages began to blend even more, and many Old Norse words became part of English.

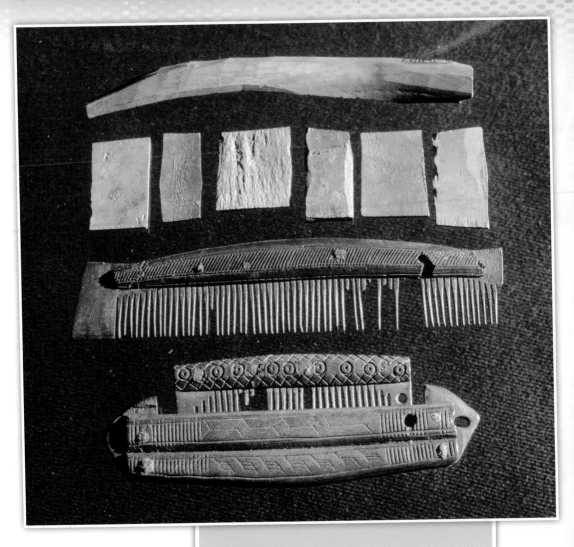

These Viking combs and hair picks were found in Ireland.

...NOW

We still use many Viking words today. For example, *egg*, *root*, and *kid* came from Old Norse, as did *sister* and *husband*, as well as *anger*, *cake*, *fellow*, *get*, *rug*, *scrub*, *skin*, *take*, and *ugly*. There are many others, including a lot of words to do with the law, farming, and trade.

Normans

At the same time some Viking armies were attacking Britain, others were invading France. In 885 CE an army of 30,000 Vikings marched on Paris. They held it for two months, but were defeated. Instead, they settled down to farm in Normandy, in northern France. They became known as Normans and began to speak French and to take on French customs.

During the Viking battle at Suffolk in 869 CE, Vikings attacked and murdered the British King Edmund.

Berserkers

Berserkers were fierce Viking warriors who howled and bit their shields before battle. They believed that their anger gave them strength.

THEN...

Fear of Viking raids forced people throughout Europe to unite into nations. According to experts, this was a major change in the history of Europe. Small kingdoms had a difficult time defending themselves, but when they joined together they became stronger. In England, the rule of William the Conqueror halted further Viking attacks.

The Danelaw

By 885 CE all of northeast England was under Viking control. This area became known as the Danelaw, and stretched from north of York all the way to London in the south. The Danelaw followed Viking laws and customs.

Later on, a new wave of Vikings attacked and conquered England. The leaders of these new groups became kings of England. However, in 1066 the Norman duke William the Conqueror invaded Britain from across the English Channel. William became the new ruler of England.

On this map, the purple line divides England. All of the land to the northeast was called the Danelaw, and was under Viking rule.

...NOW

Although history does not tell us if this was a direct result of the Vikings, this pattern of large, powerful nations continues today. For example, the countries in Britain joined to become the United Kingdom. And in North America, the colonies found strength in joining together to form one nation, the United States. Larger nations are better able to defend themselves and to grow strong.

What New Worlds Did the Vikings Explore?

The Vikings were forced to look for new lands to settle, because they were running out of good farmland at home. They were helped in this by changes in the climate. The weather became warmer than it had been in earlier centuries. This meant that the Vikings could explore new lands for a longer part of the year.

Iceland

By 870 CE the Vikings had moved farther west to Iceland. Even though farming was difficult in the cold, windy island, the settlements there grew rapidly. By 930 CE there were 30,000 people. A hundred years later, this figure had doubled to 60,000.

In Iceland, the Vikings established a **thing** to make and enforce laws. It became known as the *Althing*, and it still survives today as Iceland's national parliament.

Furs for nuts

Greenland's Viking settlers traded polar bear skins, walrus ivory, and furs for timber, tools, and special treats like raisins and nuts.

THEN...

Some experts call the Vikings the first oceanographers. Viking settlers used ocean currents to decide where to build towns and farms. In 874 CE, Ingólfur Arnarson threw wooden pillars overboard as he approached Iceland. He made his home where the wood landed (present-day Reykjavik, Iceland's capital). He knew that the ocean currents that guided the wood to land would also help ships find their way.

Greenland

In 982 CE the Viking Eric the Red set sail westward from Iceland. He saw a new land covered with ice. He called his discovery Greenland. It was colder than Iceland and it was not green, but he hoped that naming it Greenland would encourage others to join his settlement. The first settlers built dairy and sheep farms. Under Eric's leadership, Greenland's population reached 3,000.

This modern painting shows Eric the Red setting sail for Greenland with the crew of his Viking longship.

...NOW

Today, ships still use ocean currents to cut fuel costs. For example, a major shipping company in Japan tracks ocean currents. Then it guides its fleet of large oil carriers into the currents to save fuel.

North America

When Leif Eriksson, son of Erik the Red, heard rumors of an unexplored land to the west, he set off to find it. He reached Labrador, in Canada, sometime between 997 and 1003 CE. He called it *Markland*, or "Forest Land," and settled there for the winter.

Viking sagas tell of four other journeys to North America between 1000 and 1030 CE. Vikings settled at L'Anse aux Meadows in Newfoundland, Canada. They used it as a base while exploring the North Atlantic coast. The land was excellent for farming and timber, but the small band of Vikings could not defend themselves against the large numbers of Native Americans who already lived there. They returned to Iceland.

The Vikings called the Native Americans *skraelings*, which may have meant "screamers" or "screaming weaklings." However, the Native Americans were actually strong and frightening. One of the first meetings between the Vikings and *skraelings* ended in a deadly battle. The Vikings killed eight Native Americans. The *skraelings* fought back and killed the Viking leader.

The first Norwegian-American

Snorri Thorfinnsson, who was born between 1004 and 1013 CE in L'Anse aux Meadows, is thought to be the first European born in North America. When he was a child, his family returned to Iceland. Snorri Thorfinnsson became an important Icelandic leader.

THEN...

Wherever the Vikings went, they settled down. Warriors would marry local women and have families. Their children often looked like them, so Viking features were passed on to their **descendants**.

Several Viking accounts tell of battles between Viking warriors and Native Americans.

Many people in the United Kingdom are descended from Vikings. It is thought that up to 50 percent of people in some parts of northeast England might have a Viking **ancestor**. There are probably the same number of Viking descendants in Ireland and Scotland, too.

Russia and the East

While Vikings from Denmark and Norway headed west and south, the Swedes traveled east. Most Swedish Vikings were settlers and traders, not pirates. In 858 CE they captured present-day Kiev and Novgorod. From here, they spread into neighboring villages. These Swedish settlers were called the Rus.

At first the Rus were outsiders, but soon they began marrying people from the area, speaking their language, and even taking their names.

Traders

Some Swedish Vikings set up farms in Russia. Others began trading. Viking traders traveled 800 kilometers (500 miles) along the Dnieper River to the Black Sea. They crossed the sea to Constantinople, which is now known as Istanbul and is the capital of Turkey. The markets in Constantinople had riches from all over Asia, such as spices, silks, and jewelry. The Vikings took their own goods there to sell.

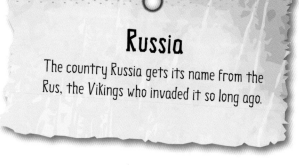

Russia
The country Russia gets its name from the Rus, the Vikings who invaded it so long ago.

THEN...

Viking trade routes stretched from Greenland in the west to Turkey in the east. Traders carried goods and information all along their routes. They showed people things they had never dreamed of before. For example, a small, bronze Buddha statue from India has been found in faraway Sweden!

Here, Viking goods are being loaded onto a trading ship, known as a knarr. They would be transported to distant lands for trading.

...NOW

Today, we depend on worldwide trade. Goods made in China are sold all over the world. Japanese cars can be bought in Europe. African coffee is used everywhere. Trade is greater and faster today than it was in the **Viking Age**, but we like foreign goods just as much as the Vikings did! Even though the Vikings probably did not invent the concept of global trade, they no doubt had a huge influence on it throughout history.

Where Are the Vikings Today?

The Vikings are not forgotten today. We use Old Norse words every day and live in cities first built by the Vikings. We may know people who are the **descendants** of Vikings, or be descended from them ourselves.

Celebrating the Vikings

Viking stories still capture our imaginations. Children and adults enjoy dressing up as Vikings. **Reenactment** societies all over the world hold pretend battles. People wear Viking clothing and carry axes and swords. No one gets hurt. It is just for fun!

This photograph shows the celebration of Up Helly Aa, a Scottish fire festival. People burn Viking-style ships, dress as Vikings, and sing songs in Old Norse.

This Swedish soccer fan has dressed up to support his team. "Vikings" is a popular team name in many sports, including the football team the Minnesota Vikings.

Horned helmets

Many people think that the Vikings wore helmets with big horns on them. Actually, they did not! Warriors wore a sheepskin cap with an iron helmet over it. A metal piece came down in front to cover the warrior's nose.

Key Dates

Here is an outline of important moments in the history and culture of the Vikings:

14,000 years ago	Settlers move into Scandinavia from the east
4,000 years ago	Ancient Scandinavians begin farming
500 CE	Scandinavians trade with other Europeans
700	The Vikings excel at shipbuilding
793	A raid on Lindisfarne marks the beginning of the **Viking Age**
832	Ireland is raided three times in one month
841	Vikings conquer Ulster and found a settlement that will become Dublin
858	Swedish Vikings take over Novgorod and Kiev

866	A Viking army captures York, and some Vikings begin settling down in the lands they have invaded
870–930	Vikings settle in Iceland
885–86	Vikings attack Paris
900	Vikings settle in northwest England
907	Vikings reach Constantinople and begin trading with the city
911	Vikings settle in Normandy
940–954	The Vikings and the English fight over York
986	Eric the Red leads the settlement of Greenland
Late 900s	Voyages to North America begin
990–1030	Vikings settle in present-day Canada
1066	The Battle of Hastings marks the end of the Viking era

Glossary

ancestor past member of a family. Many people today have Viking ancestors.

BCE short for "Before the Common Era." BCE is used for all the years before year 1.

CE short for "Common Era." CE is used for all the years after year 1.

cleat metal strip designed to protect against slipping. Boots with cleats help us walk on ice.

descendant member of a family who can be traced back to a member in the past. The Vikings left descendants wherever they settled.

forge blacksmith's workshop. Viking farms often had a forge.

jury group of people chosen to make a decision. Viking juries judged criminals and solved problems.

lapstrake ship built with overlapping boards. Viking boats were lapstrakes.

monastery place where monks live and worship. Vikings raided monasteries looking for gold.

pagan person who believes in more than one god. Vikings were pagans.

reenactment perform something again. Reenactment societies perform Viking battles in modern times.

rivet metal pin used to hold pieces together. Viking boat builders used rivets to hold the wood together.

thing assembly held once or twice a year in Viking settlements. Viking laws were made at *things*.

Viking Age period between 800 to 1100 CE, when the Vikings raided, explored, and traded all over the world. The Viking Age was a time of great change.

Find Out More

Books

Binns, Tristan Boyer. *Ancient Civilizations: The Vikings.*
    Minneapolis: Compass Point, 2006.

Hewitt, Sally. *Starting History: The Vikings.* North Mankato,
    Minn.: Smart Apple Media, 2008.

Lassieur, Allison. *Warriors of History: The Vikings.*
    North Mankato, Minn.: Capstone, 2007.

Websites

www.mnh.si.edu/vikings/start.html
Find out more about the Viking exploration of Greenland and
North America on this useful website.

www.pbs.org/wgbh/nova/vikings/
This website has lots of information on Viking history. You can
explore a Viking village and learn how to write your name in the
Viking alphabet.

A place to visit

L'Anse aux Meadows National Historic Site of Canada
P.O. Box 70
St-Lunaire-Griquet Newfoundland and Labrador A0K 2X0
Canada
www.pc.gc.ca/voyage-travel/pv-vp/itm1-/page14_e.asp

Index